HYMNS
FOR ACCORDION

ISBN 978-1-5400-2787-0

Visit Hal Leonard Online at
www.halleonard.com

Contact Us:
Hal Leonard
7777 West Bluemound Road
Milwaukee, WI 53213
Email: info@halleonard.com

In Europe contact:
Hal Leonard Europe Limited
42 Wigmore Street
Marylebone, London, W1U 2RN
Email: info@halleonardeurope.com

In Australia contact:
Hal Leonard Australia Pty. Ltd.
4 Lentara Court
Cheltenham, Victoria, 3192 Australia
Email: info@halleonard.com.au

ALL HAIL THE POWER OF JESUS' NAME

Words by EDWARD PERRONET
Music by OLIVER HOLDEN

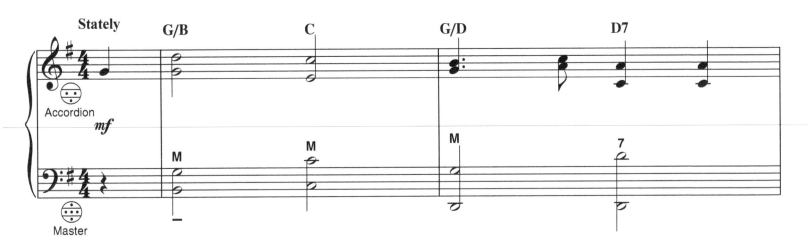

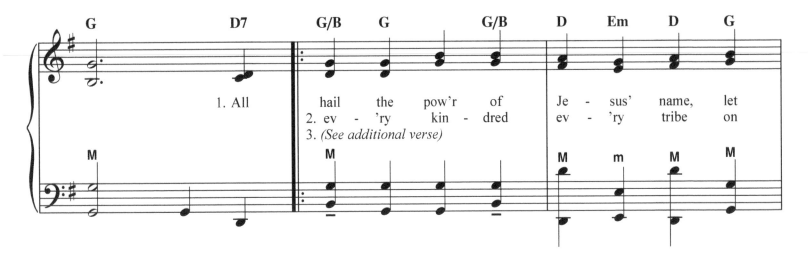

1. All hail the pow'r of Jesus' name, let
2. ev - 'ry kin - dred ev - 'ry tribe on
3. *(See additional verse)*

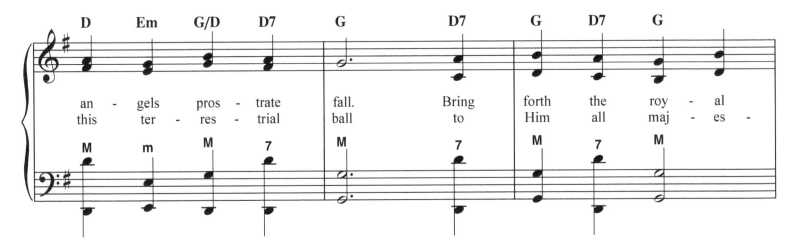

an - gels pros - trate fall. Bring forth the roy - al
this ter - res - trial ball to Him all maj - es -

5

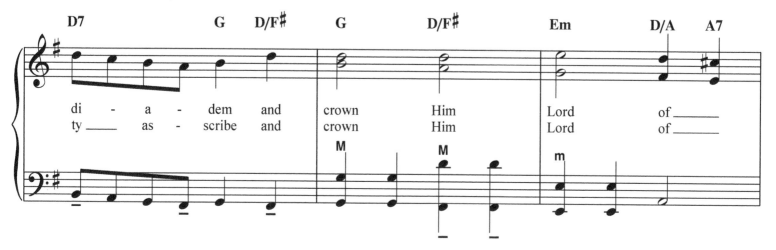

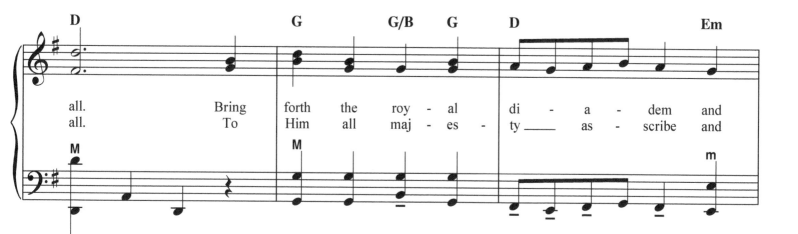

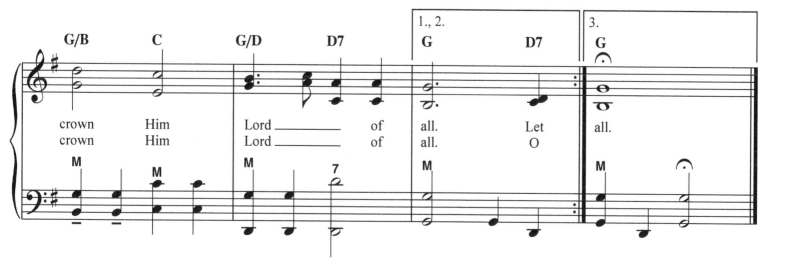

Additional Verse

3. O that with yonder sacred throng we at His feet may fall.
We'll join the everlasting song and crown Him Lord of all.
We'll join the everlasting song and crown Him Lord of all.

AMAZING GRACE

Words by JOHN NEWTON
Traditional American Melody

1. A- maz - ing __ grace how sweet the
2. grace that __ taught how my heart to
3.–5. *(See additional verses)*

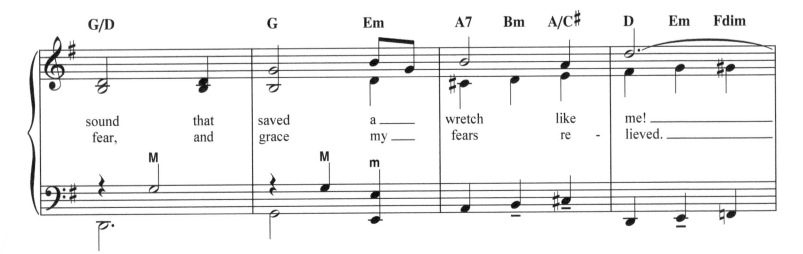

sound that saved a __ wretch like me! __
fear, and grace my __ fears re - lieved. __

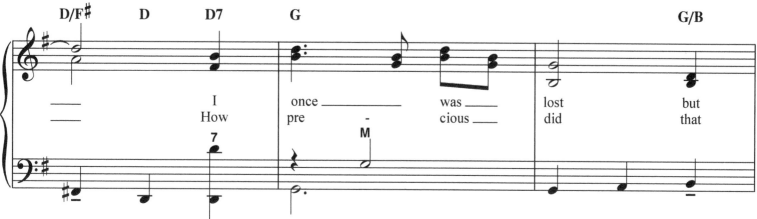

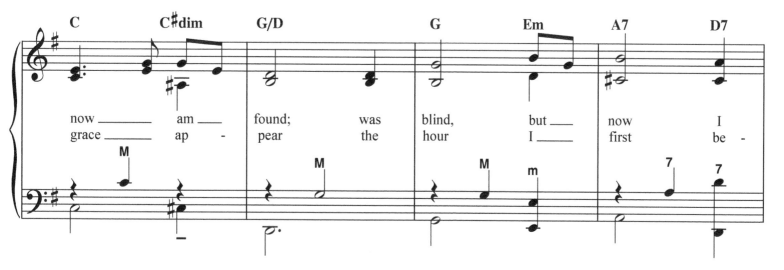

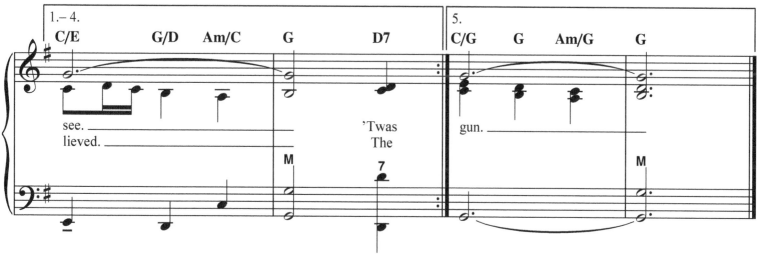

Additional Verses

3. The Lord has promised good to me;
   His word my hope secures.
   He will my shield and portion be
   As long as life endures.

4. Through many dangers, toils, and snares
   I have already come.
   'Tis grace hath brought me safe thus far,
   And grace will lead me home.

5. When we've been there ten thousand years,
   Bright shining as the sun,
   We've no less days to sing God's praise
   Than when we'd first begun.

BE THOU MY VISION

Traditional Irish
Translated by MARY E. BYRNE

1. Be thou my ___ vi - sion, O Lord of my heart;
2. Be thou my ___ wis - dom, and Thou my true word;
3. *(See additional verse)*

naught be all else to me, save that Thou art.
I ev - er with Thee and Thou with me, Lord;

9

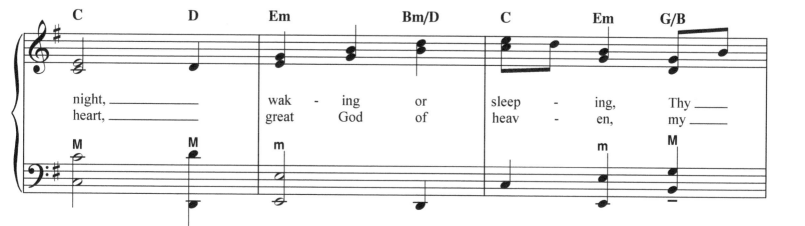

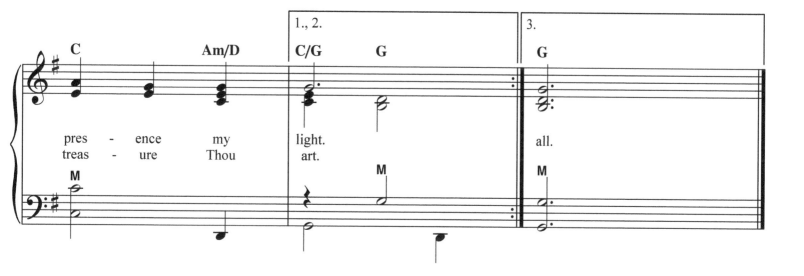

Additional Verse

3. Great God of heaven, my victory won,
May I reach heaven's joys, O bright heav'n's Sun!
Heart of my own heart, whatever befall,
Still be my vision, O ruler of all.

BEAUTIFUL SAVIOR

Words from *Munsterisch Gesangbuch*
Music adapted from Silesian Folk Tune

1. Beau - ti - ful Sav - ior! King of cre - a - tion!
2. Fair are the mead - ows, fair are the wood - lands,
3., 4. *(See additional verses)*

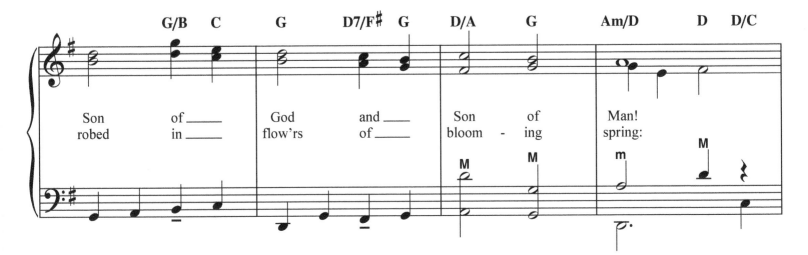

Son of ___ God and ___ Son of Man!
robed in ___ flow'rs of ___ bloom - ing spring:

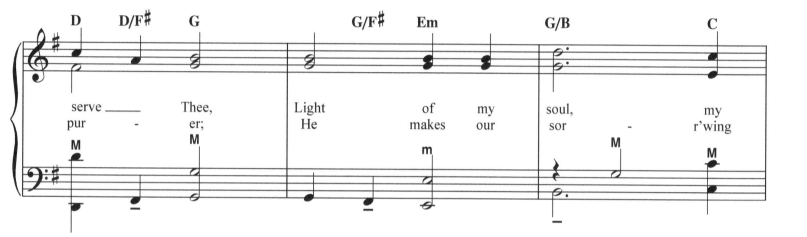

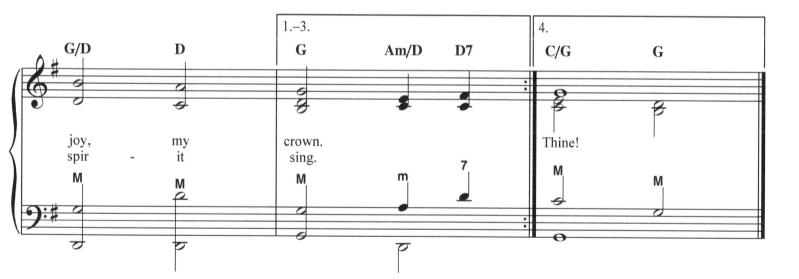

Additional Verses

3. Fair is the sunshine, Fair is the moonlight,
   Bright the sparkling stars on high:
   Jesus shines brighter, Jesus shines purer
   Than all the angels in the sky.

4. Beautiful Savior! Lord of the nations!
   Son of God and Son of Man!
   Glory and honor, Praise, adoration,
   Now and forevermore be Thine!

COME, THOU FOUNT OF EVERY BLESSING

Words by ROBERT ROBINSON
Music from John Wyeth's *Repository of Sacred Music*

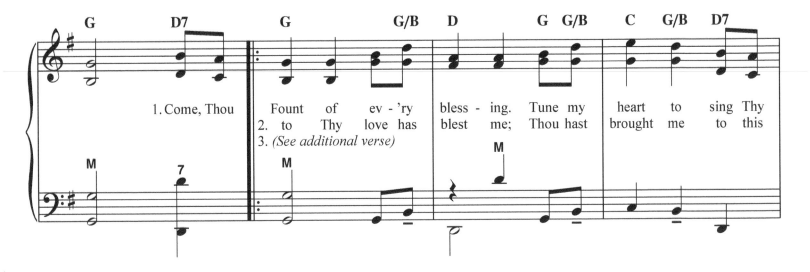

1. Come, Thou Fount of ev-'ry bless-ing. Tune my heart to sing Thy
2. to Thy love has blest me; Thou hast brought me to this
3. *(See additional verse)*

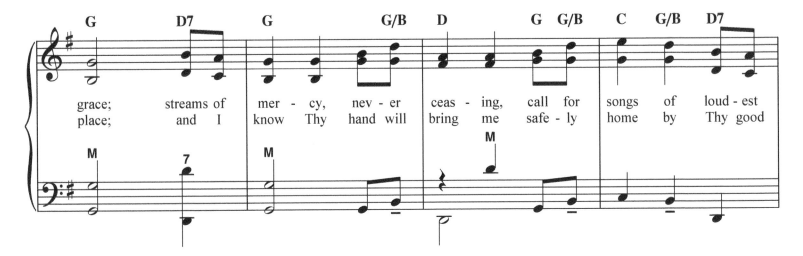

grace; streams of mer-cy, nev-er ceas-ing, call for songs of loud-est
place; and I know Thy hand will bring me safe-ly home by Thy good

praise. Teach me ___ some me - lo - dious son - net sung by ___
grace. Je - sus ___ sought me when a stran - ger, wan - d'ring ___

flam - ing tongues a - bove; praise His name I'm fixed up -
from the fold of God; He, to res - cue me from

on it name of God's re - deem - ing love. Hith - er bove.
dan - ger, bought me with His pre - cious blood. O to

Additional Verse

3. O to grace how great a debtor
Daily I'm constrained to be!
Let Thy goodness, like a fetter,
Bind my wand'ring heart to Thee;
Prone to wander, Lord I feel it,
Prone to leave the God I love;
Here's my heart, O take and seal it;
Seal it for Thy courts above.

CROWN HIM WITH MANY CROWNS

Words by MATTHEW BRIDGES
and GODFREY THRING
Music by GEORGE JOB ELVEY

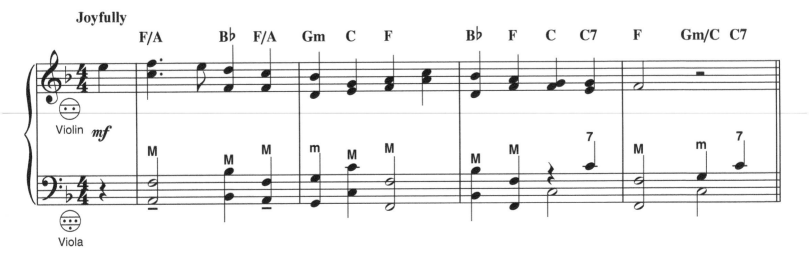

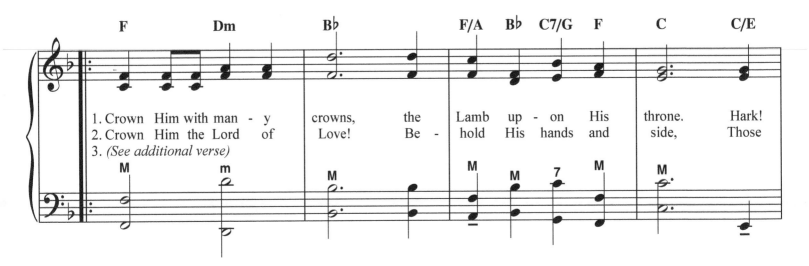

1. Crown Him with man - y crowns, the Lamb up - on His throne. Hark!
2. Crown Him the Lord of Love! Be - hold His hands and side, Those
3. (See additional verse)

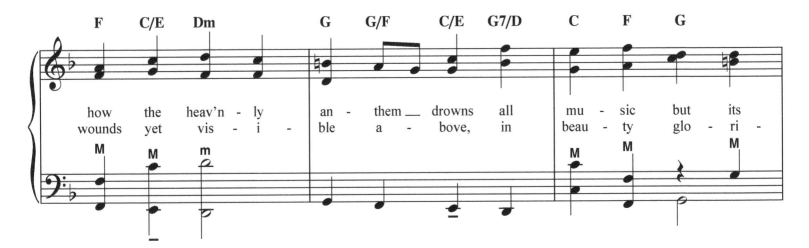

how the heav'n - ly an - them drowns all mu - sic but its
wounds yet vis - i - ble a - bove, in beau - ty glo - ri -

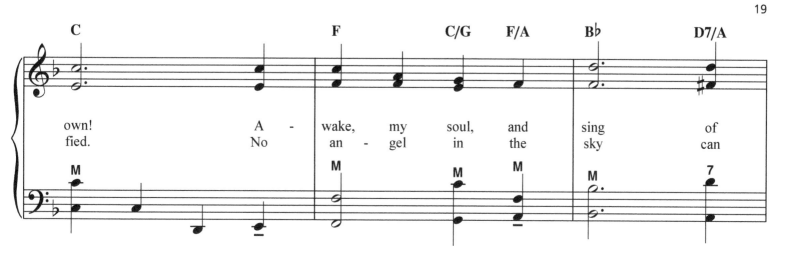

own!
fied.

A -
No

wake,
an -

my
gel

soul,
in

and
the

sing
sky

of
can

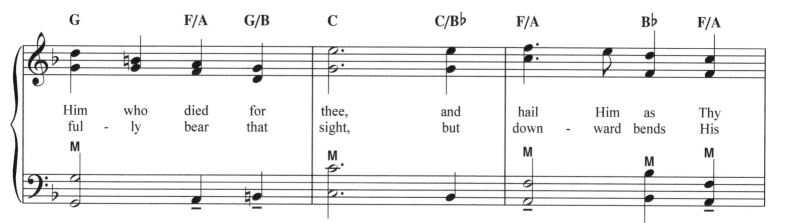

Him
ful

who
-

died
ly

for
bear

that

thee,
sight,

and
but

hail
down

Him
-

as
ward

bends

Thy
His

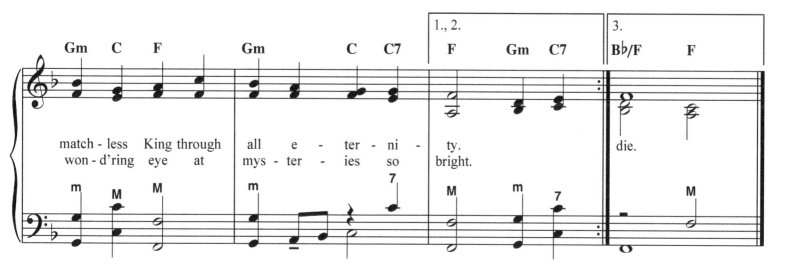

match - less
won - d'ring

King through
eye   at

all
mys -

e - ter - ni -
ter - ies   so

ty.
bright.

die.

Additional Verse

3. Crown Him the Lord of Life, Who triumphed o'er the grave,
   And rose victorious in the strife For those He came to save.
   His glories now we sing, Who died and rose on high,
   Who died eternal life to bring And lives that death may die.

FOR THE BEAUTY OF THE EARTH

Words by FOLLIOT S. PIERPOINT
Music by CONRAD KOCHER

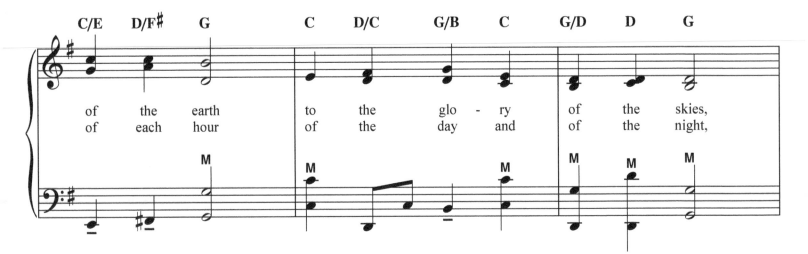

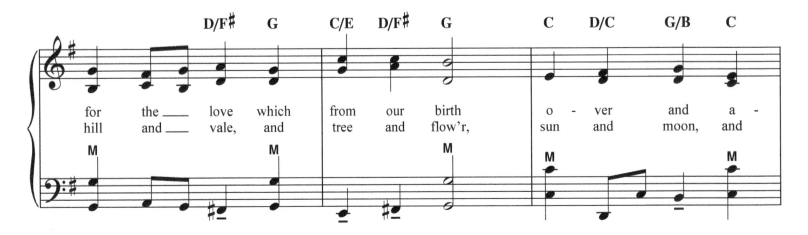

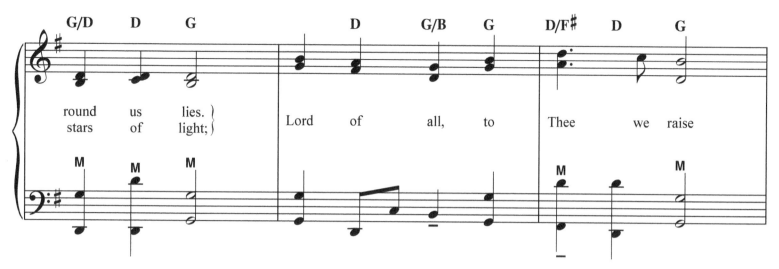

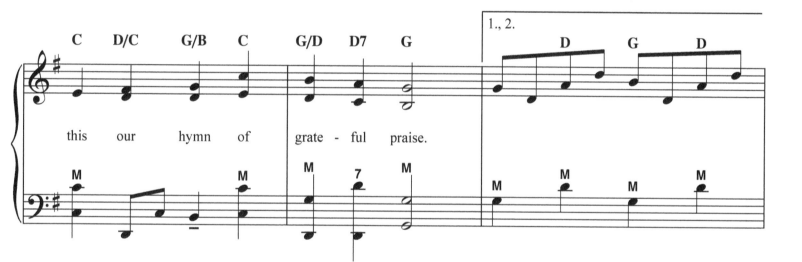

Additional Verse

3. For the joy of human love, brother, sister, parent, child,
   Friends on earth and friends above, for all gentle thoughts and mild;
   Lord of all, to Thee we raise this our hymn of grateful praise.

HOLY, HOLY, HOLY

Text by REGINALD HEBER
Music by JOHN B. DYKES

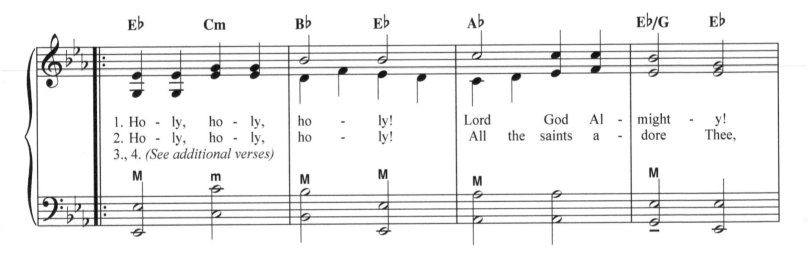

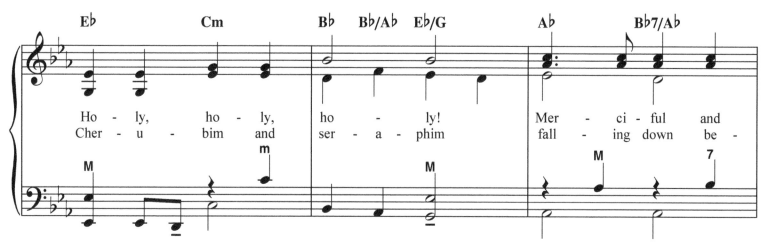

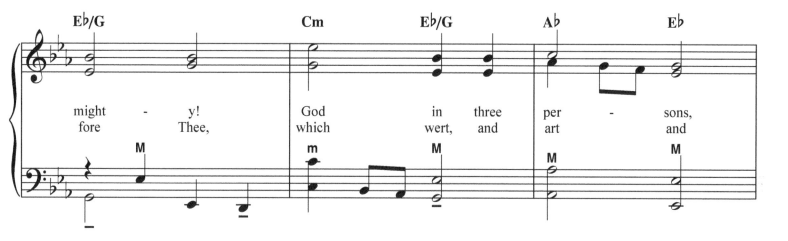

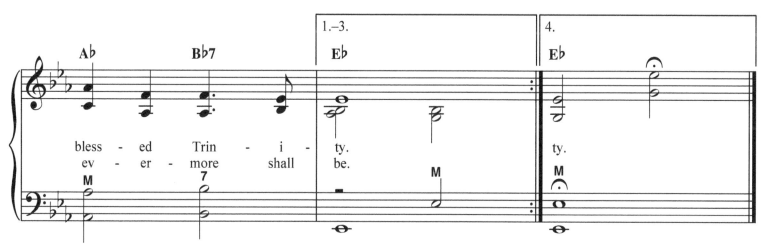

Additional Verses

3. Holy, holy, holy! Though the darkness hide Thee,
Though the eye of sinful man Thy glory may not see,
Only Thou are holy; there is none beside Thee,
Perfect in pow'r, in love and purity.

4. Holy, holy, holy! Lord God Almighty!
All Thy works shall praise Thy name in earth and sky and sea.
Holy, holy, holy! Merciful and mighty!
God in three persons, blessed Trinity.

I LOVE TO TELL THE STORY

Words by CATHERINE HANKEY
Music by WILLIAM G. FISCHER

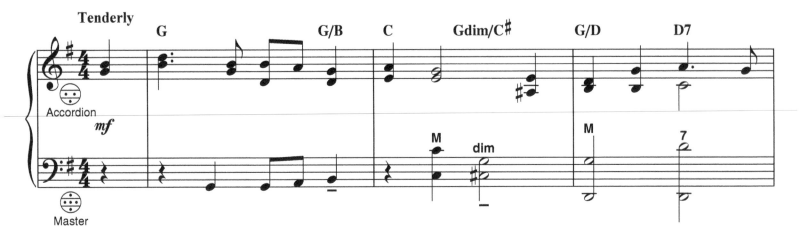

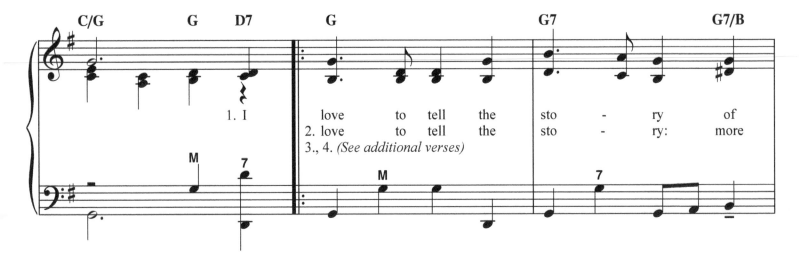

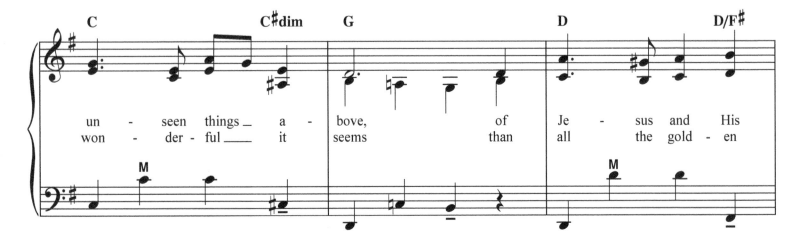

25

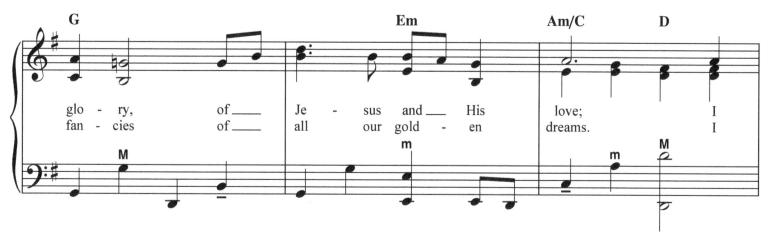

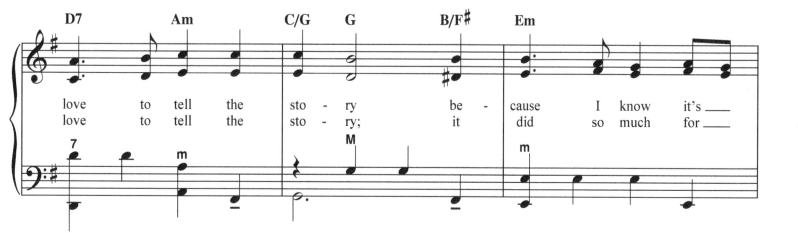

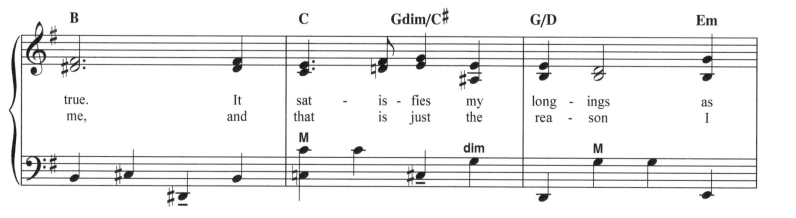

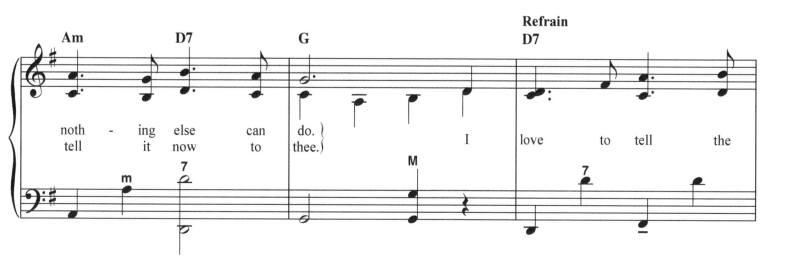

26

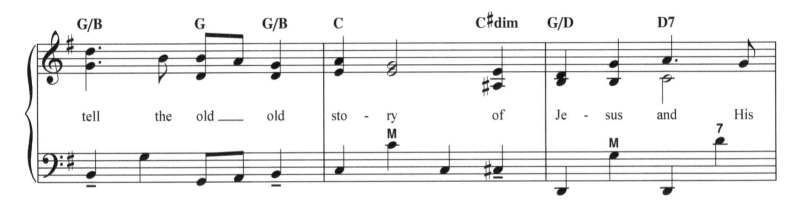

Additional Verses

3. I love to tell the story 'tis pleasant to repeat
   What seems each time I tell it, more wonderfully sweet.
   I love to tell the story for some have never heard
   The message of salvation from God's Own holy word.
   Refrain

4. I love to tell the story; for those who know it best
   Seem hungering and thirsting to hear it like the rest.
   And when, in scenes of glory, I sing the new song,
   'Twill be the old, old story that I loved so long.
   Refrain

THE OLD RUGGED CROSS

Words and Music by
Rev. GEORGE BENNARD

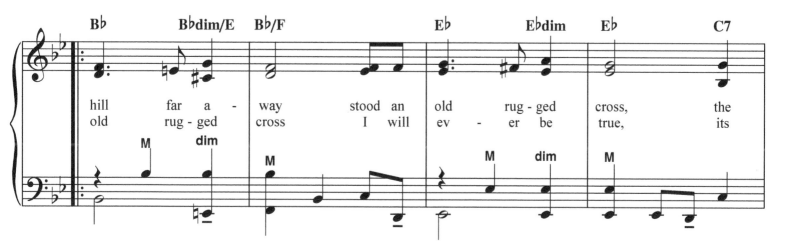

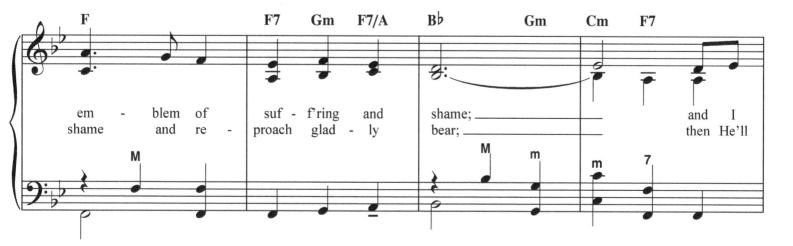

28

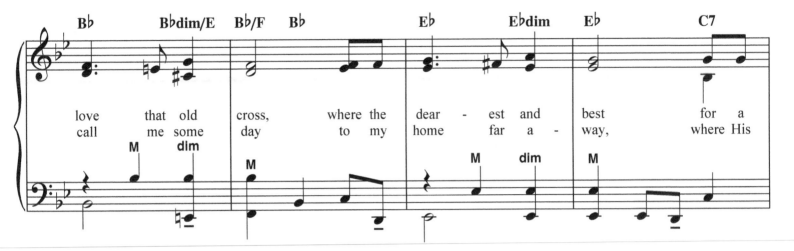

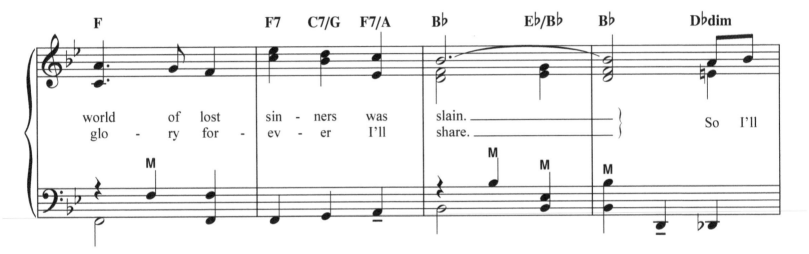

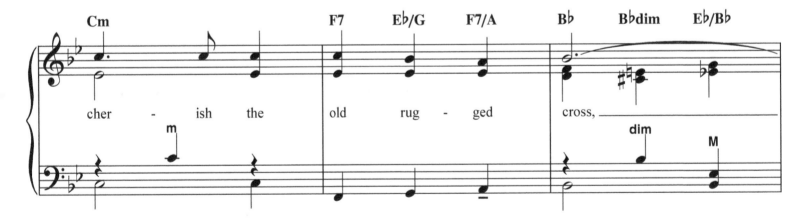

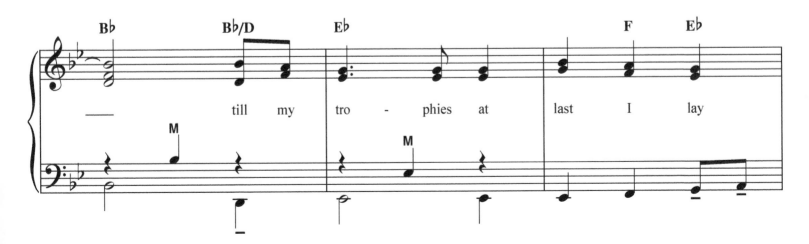

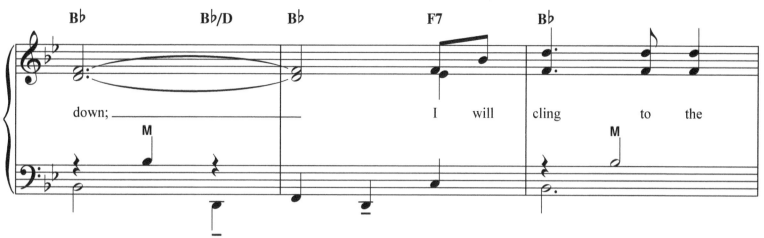

down; _____ I will cling to the

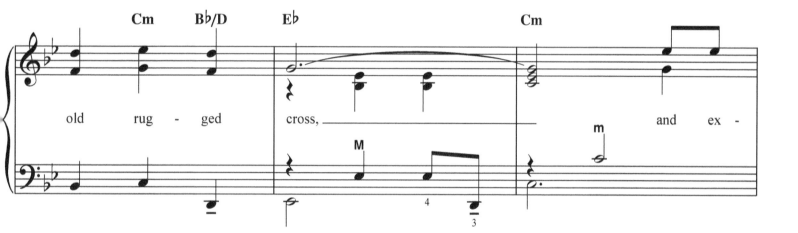

old rug - ged cross, _____ and ex -

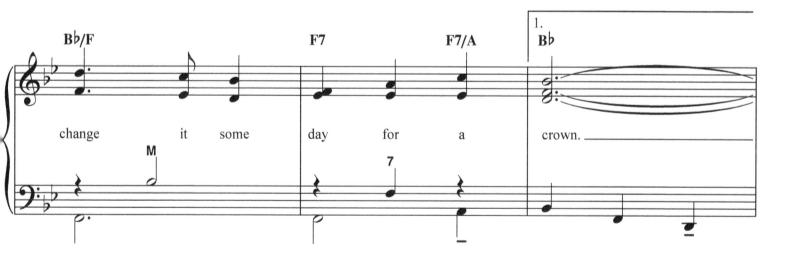

change it some day for a crown. _____

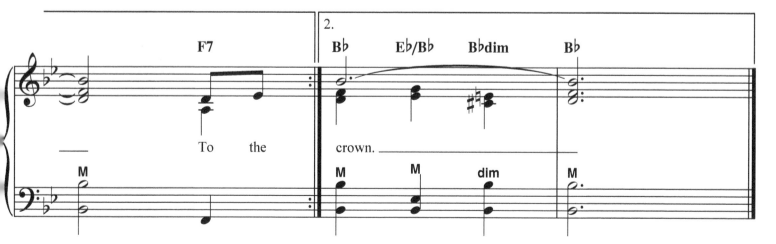

To the crown. _____

I NEED THEE EVERY HOUR

Words by ANNIE S. HAWKS
Music by ROBERT LOWRY

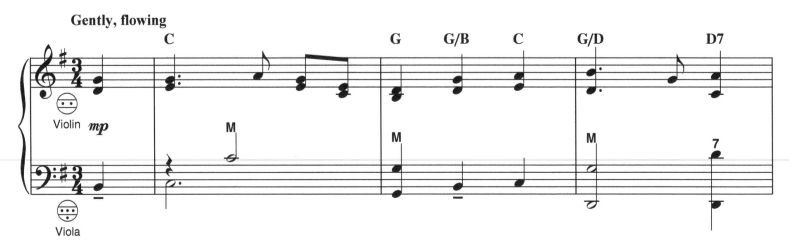

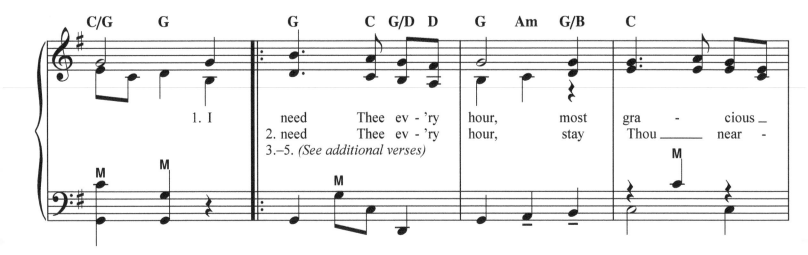

1. I need Thee ev - 'ry hour, most gra - cious
2. need Thee ev - 'ry hour, most stay Thou near -
3.–5. *(See additional verses)*

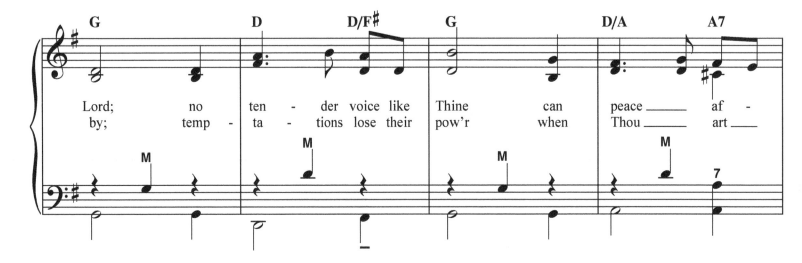

Lord; no ten - der voice like Thine can peace af -
by; temp - ta - tions lose their pow'r can when Thou art

31

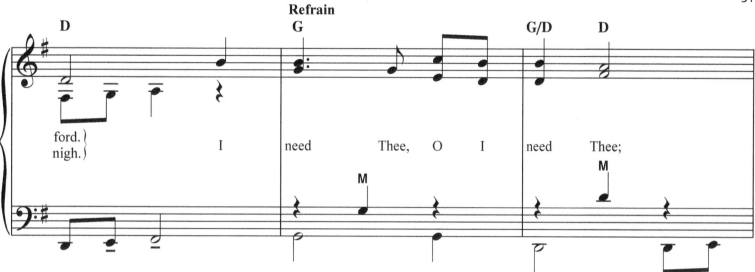

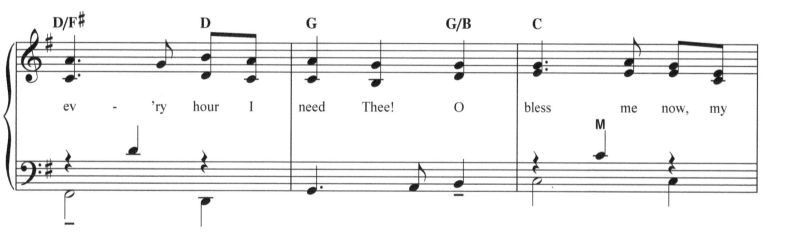

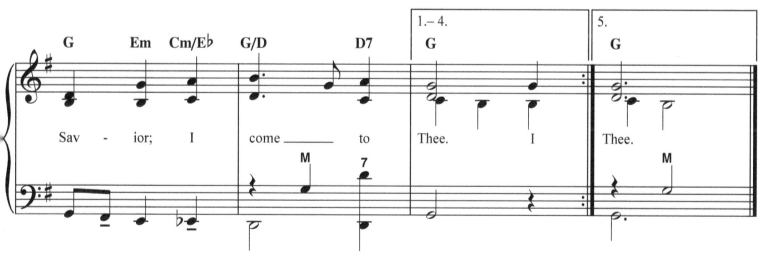

Additional Verses

3. I need Thee ev'ry hour; in joy or pain;
   Come quickly and abide or life is vain.
   Refrain

4. I need Thee ev'ry hour; teach me Thy will,
   And Thy rich promises in me fulfill.
   Refrain

5. I need Thee ev'ry hour, most Holy One;
   O make me Thine indeed, Thou blessed Son.
   Refrain

I SURRENDER ALL

Words by J.W. VAN DEVENTER
Music by W.S. WEEDEN

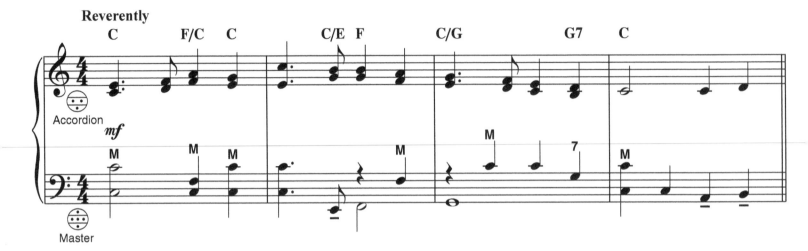

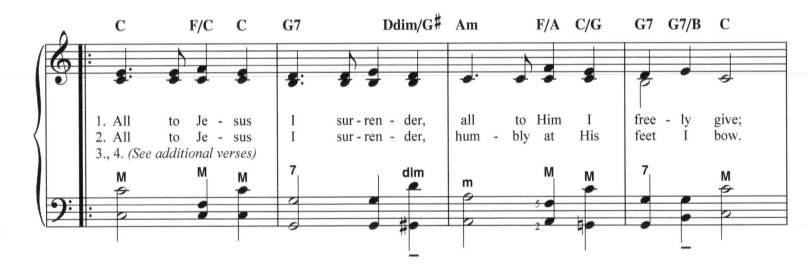

1. All to Je - sus I sur - ren - der, all to Him I free - ly give;
2. All to Je - sus I sur - ren - der, hum - bly at His feet I bow.
3., 4. *(See additional verses)*

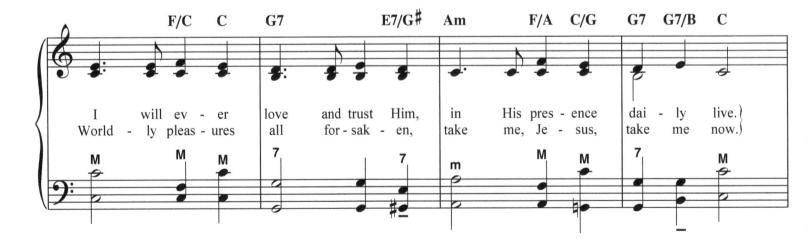

I will ev - er love and trust Him, in His pres - ence dai - ly live.)
World - ly pleas - ures all for - sak - en, take me, Je - sus, take me now.)

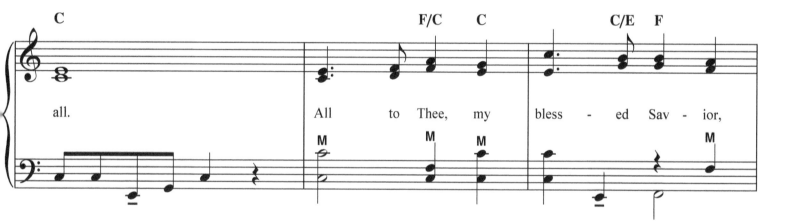

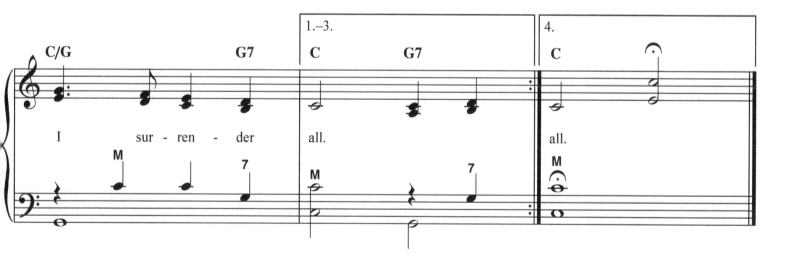

Additional Verses

3. All to Jesus I surrender, make me, Savior, wholly Thine.
   Let me feel the Holy Spirit, truly know that Thou art mine.
   Refrain

4. All to Jesus I surrender, Lord, I give myself to Thee;
   Fill me with Thy love and power, let Thy blessing fall on me.
   Refrain

IN THE GARDEN

Words and Music by
C. AUSTIN MILES

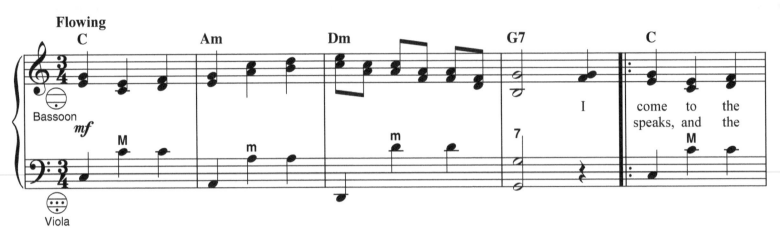

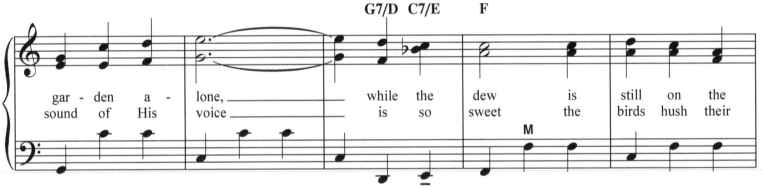

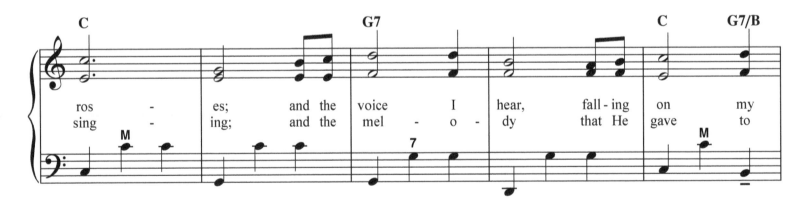

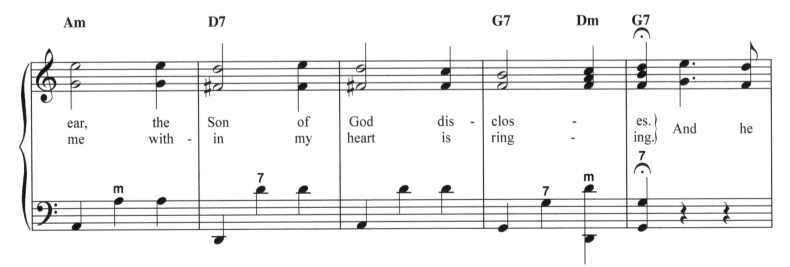

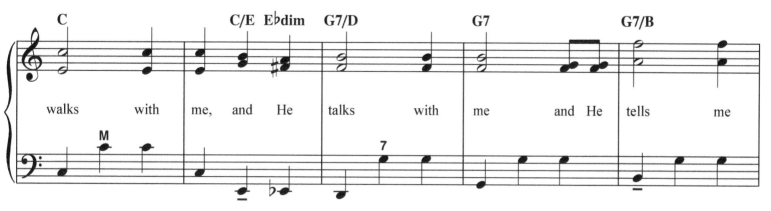

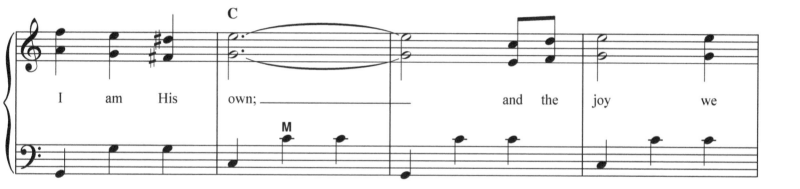

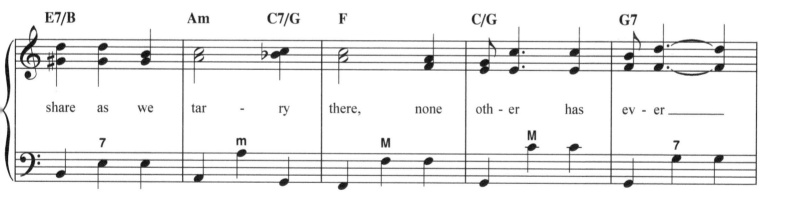

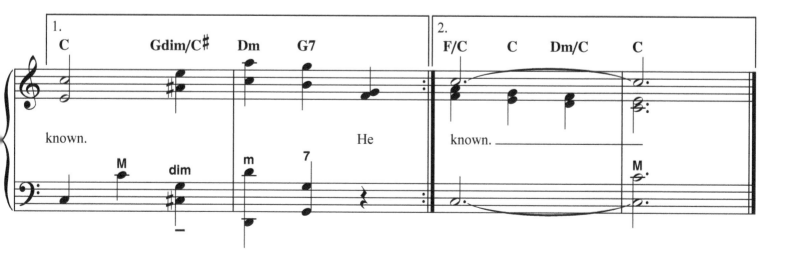

IT IS WELL WITH MY SOUL

Words by HORATIO G. SPAFFORD
Music by PHILIP P. BLISS

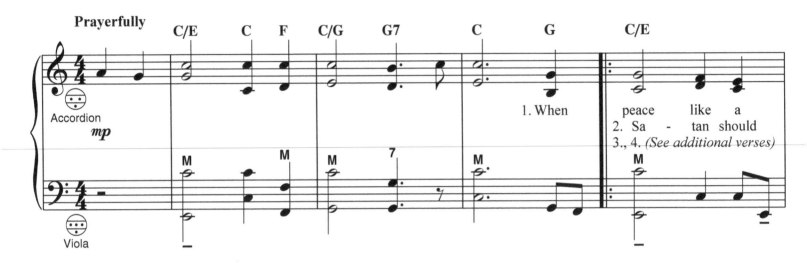

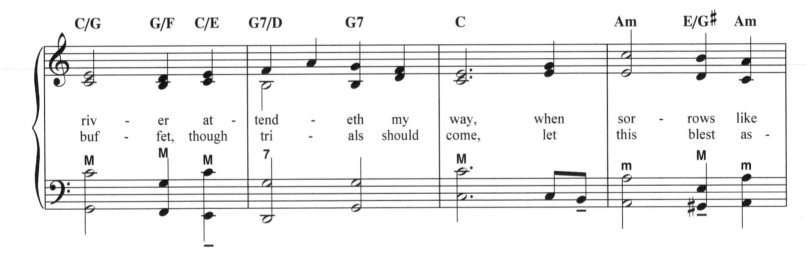

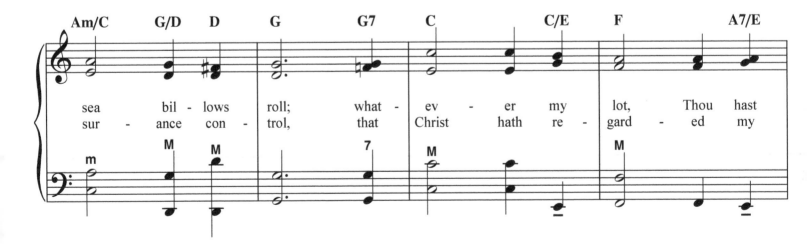

37

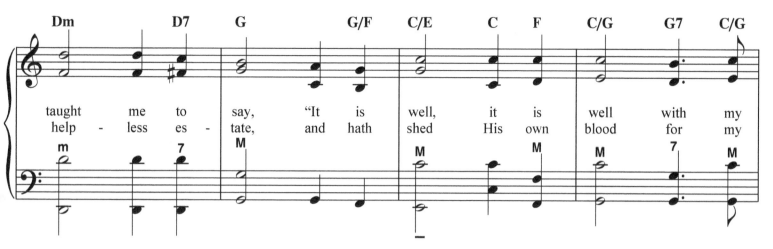

Additional Verses

3. My sin, O, the bliss of this glorious thought
   My sin not in part, but the whole,
   Is nailed to the cross, and I bear it no more,
   Praise the Lord, praise the Lord, O my soul!
   Refrain

4. And, Lord, haste the day when the faith shall be sight,
   The clouds be rolled back as a scroll,
   The trump shall resound and the Lord shall descend,
   Even so, it is well with my soul.
   Refrain

JUST A CLOSER WALK WITH THEE

Traditional
Arranged by KENNETH MORRIS

Chorus

Just a clos - er walk with Thee, grant it, Je - sus, is my

plea. _ Dai - ly walk-ing close to Thee, _____ let it

be, dear Lord, let it be. be.

Additional Verse

3. When my feeble life is o'er,
   Time for me will be no more.
   Guide me gently, safely o'er
   To Thy kingdom shore, to Thy shore.
   Chorus

A MIGHTY FORTRESS IS OUR GOD

Words and Music by
MARTIN LUTHER

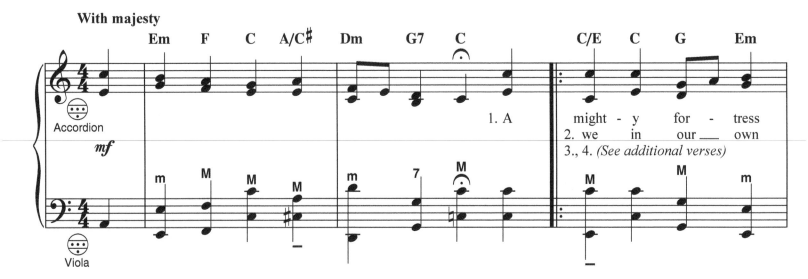

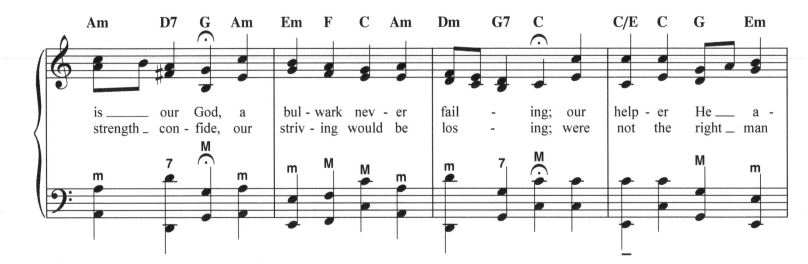

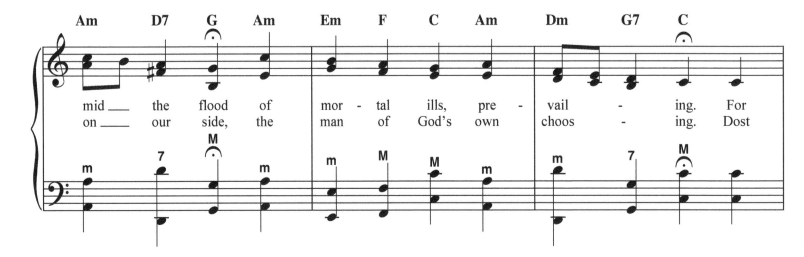

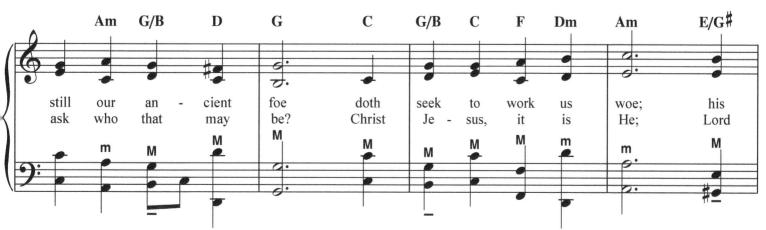

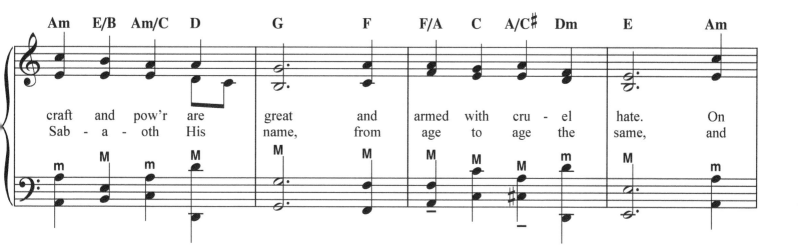

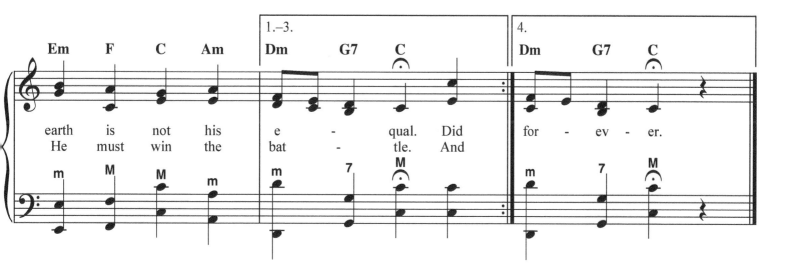

Additional Verses

3. And though this world, with devils filled,
   Should threaten to undo us;
   We will not fear, for God hath willed
   His truth to triumph through us;
   The Prince of darkness grim,
   We tremble not for him;
   His rage we can endure,
   For lo! His doom is sure,
   One little word shall fell him.

4. That word above all earthly pow'rs,
   No thanks to them abideth,
   The Spirit and the gifts are ours
   Through Him who with us sideth;
   Let goods and kindred go,
   This mortal life also;
   The body they may kill;
   God's truth abideth still,
   His kingdom is forever.

MY FAITH LOOKS UP TO THEE

Words by RAY PALMER
Music by LOWELL MASON

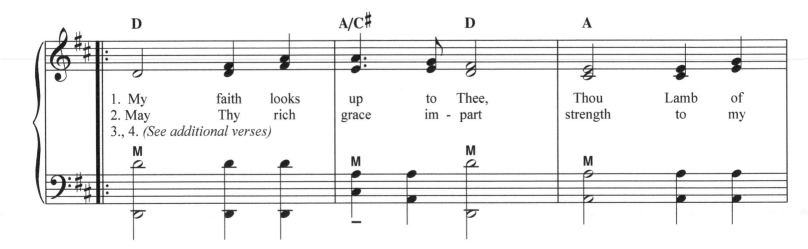

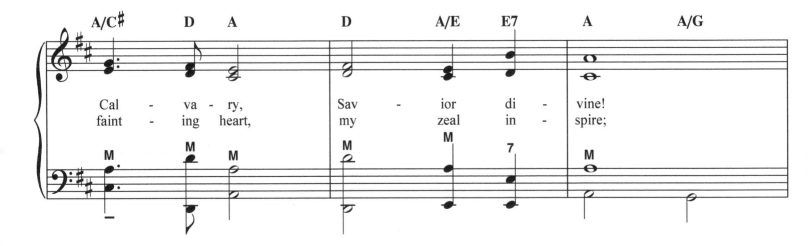

Additional Verses

3. While life's dark maze I tread
   And griefs around me spread,
   Be Thou my guide;
   Bid darkness turn to day,
   Wipe sorrow's tears away,
   Nor let me over stray
   From Thee aside.

4. When ends life's passing dream,
   When death's cold, threat'ning stream
   Shall o'er me roll,
   Blest Savior, then, in love,
   Fear and distrust remove;
   O lift me safe above,
   A ransomed soul.

NEARER, MY GOD, TO THEE

Words by SARAH F. ADAMS
Music by LOWELL MASON

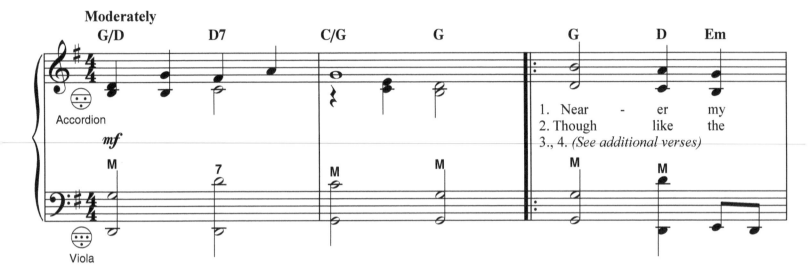

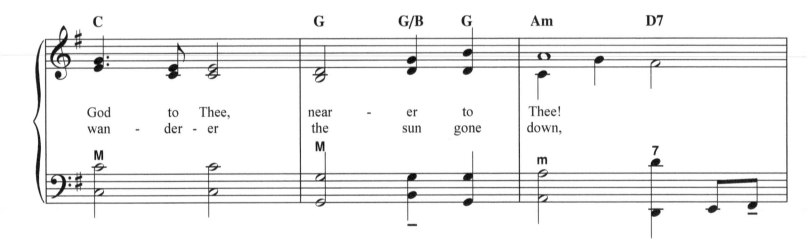

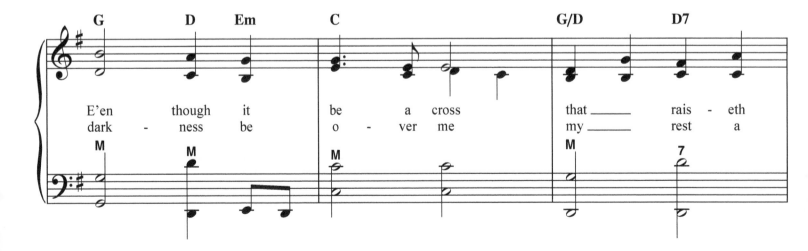

45

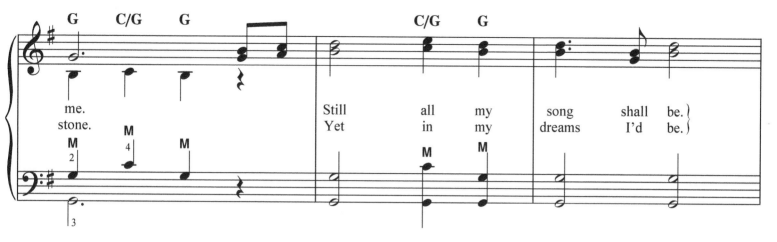

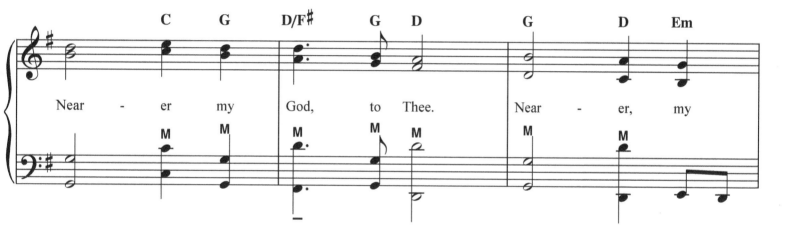

Additional Verses

3. Then with my waking thoughts
   Bright with Thy praise,
   Out of my stony griefs
   Bethel I'll raise.
   So by my woes to be,
   Nearer, my God, to Thee,
   Nearer, my God, to Thee,
   Nearer to Thee!

4. Or if on joyful wing,
   Cleaving the sky,
   Sun, moon, and stars forgot,
   Upwards I'll fly.
   Still all my song shall be,
   Nearer, my God, to Thee,
   Nearer, my God, to Thee,
   Nearer to Thee!

ROCK OF AGES

Words by AUGUSTUS M. TOPLADY
Music by THOMAS HASTINGS

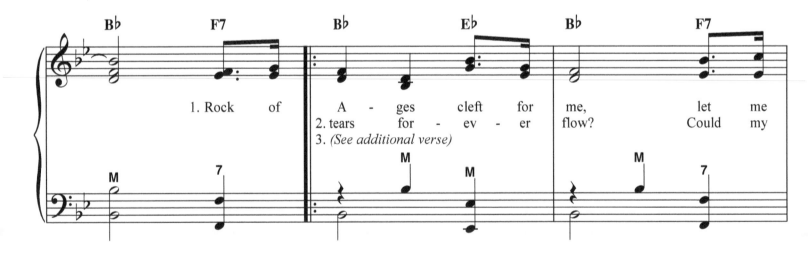

1. Rock of A - ges cleft for me, let me
2. tears for - ev - er flow? Could my
3. (See additional verse)

hide my - self in Thee. Let the wa - ter and the
zeal no lan - guor know? These for sin could not a -

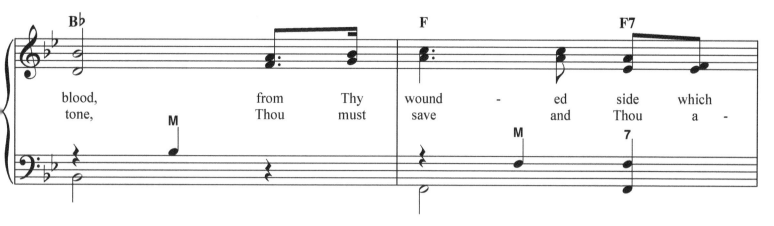

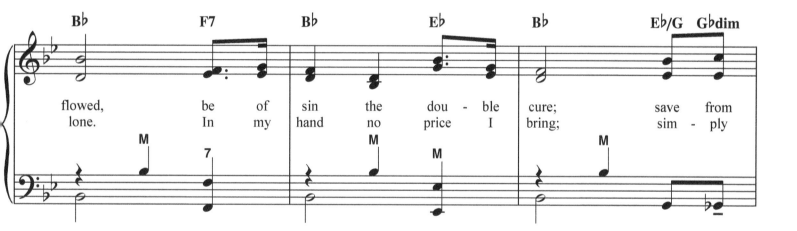

Additional Verse

3. While I draw this fleeting breath, when my eyes shall close in death,
When I rise to worlds unknown, and behold Thee on Thy throne,
Rock of Ages cleft for me, let me hide myself in Thee.

SAVIOR, LIKE A SHEPHERD LEAD US

Words from *Hymns For the Young*
Attributed to DOROTHY A. THRUPP
Music by WILLIAM B. BRADURY

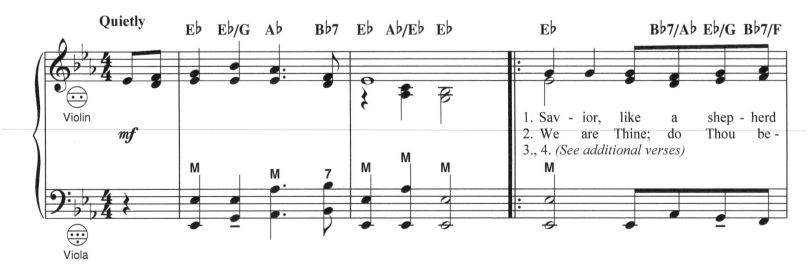

1. Sav - ior, like a shep - herd
2. We are Thine; do Thou be -
3., 4. *(See additional verses)*

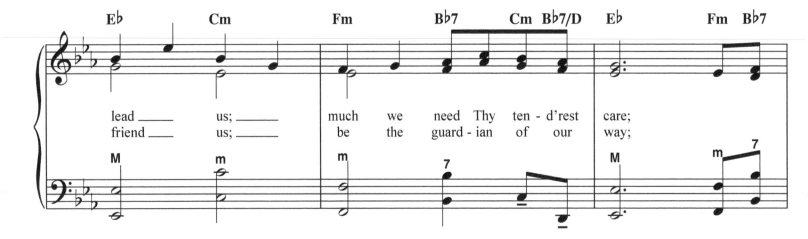

lead _____ us; _____ much we need Thy ten - d'rest care;
friend _____ us; _____ be the guard - ian of our way;

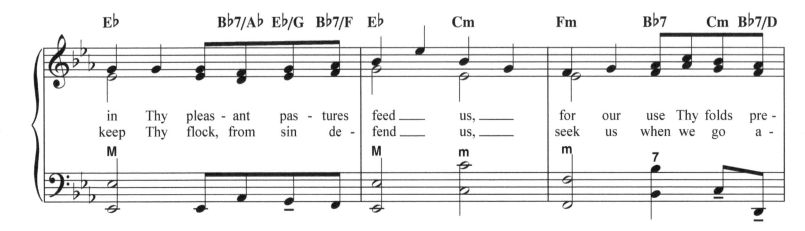

in Thy pleas - ant pas - tures feed _____ us, _____ for our use Thy folds pre -
keep Thy flock, from sin de - fend _____ us, _____ seek us when we go a -

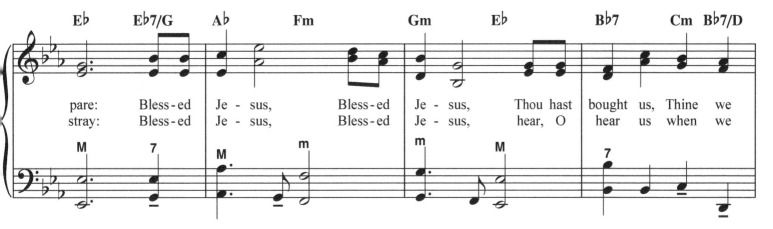

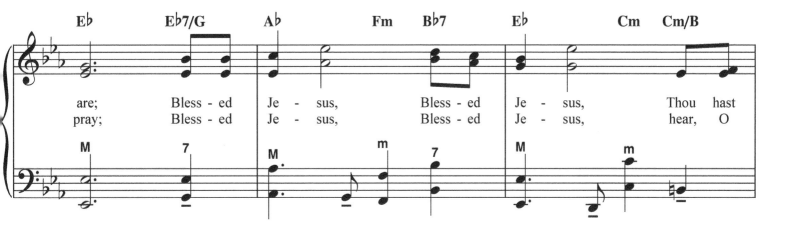

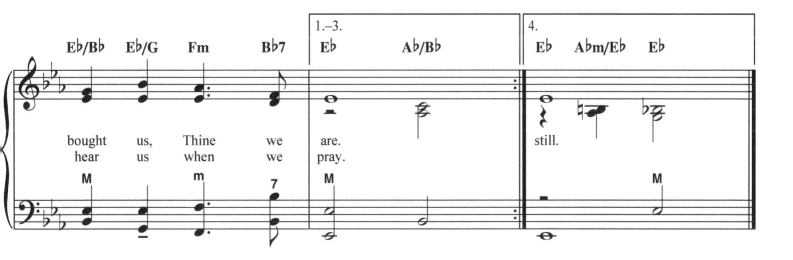

Additional Verses

3. Thou hast promised to receive us,
   Poor and sinful though we be;
   Thou hast mercy to relieve us
   Grace to cleanse and pow'r to free.
   Blessed Jesus, Blessed Jesus,
   Early let us turn to Thee;
   Blessed Jesus, Blessed Jesus,
   Early let us turn to Thee.

4. Early let us seek Thy favor,
   Early let us do Thy will;
   Blessed Lord and only Savior,
   With Thy love our bosoms fill.
   Blessed Jesus, Blessed Jesus,
   Thou hast loved us, love us still;
   Blessed Jesus, Blessed Jesus,
   Thou hast loved us love us still.

THIS IS MY FATHER'S WORLD

Words by MALTBIE D. BABCOCK
Music by FRANKLIN L. SHEPPARD

51

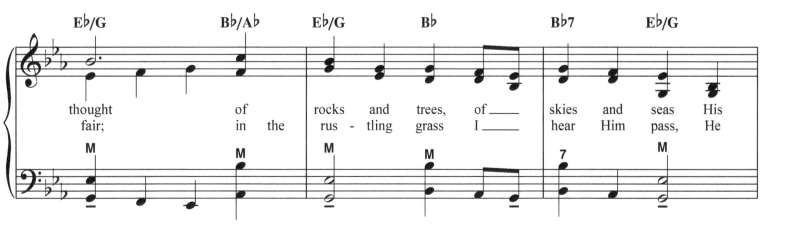

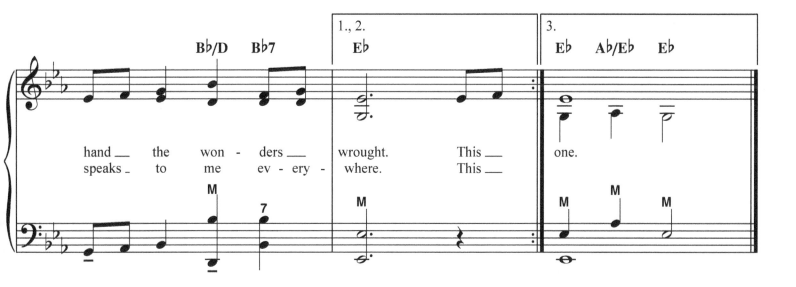

Additional Verse

3. This is my Father's world, O let me ne'er forget
   That though the wrong seems oft so strong, God is the Ruler yet.
   This is my Father's world, the battle is not done;
   Jesus, who died shall be satisfied, and earth and heav'n be one.

52

WHAT A FRIEND WE HAVE IN JESUS

Words by JOSEPH M. SCRIVEN
Music by CHARLES C. CONVERSE

1. What a friend we have in
2. Have we tri-als and temp-
3. *(See additional verse)*

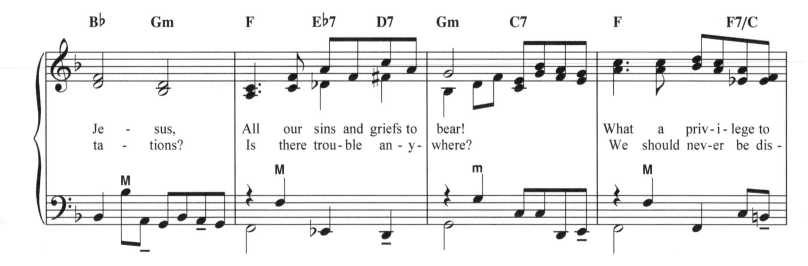

Je - sus, / ta - tions?
All our sins and griefs to / Is there trou-ble an-y-
bear! / where?
What a priv-i-lege to / We should nev-er be dis-

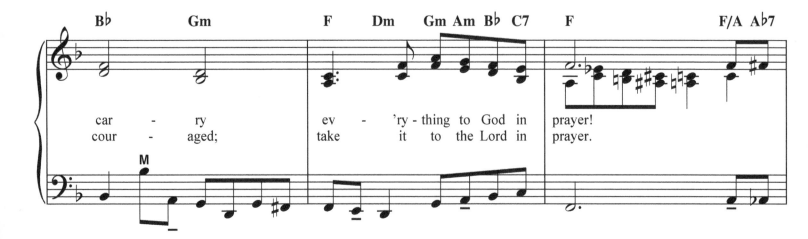

car - ry / cour - aged;
ev - 'ry-thing to God in / take it to the Lord in
prayer! / prayer.

Additional Verse

3. Are we weak and heavy-laden,
   Cumbered with a load of care?
   Precious Savior, still our refuge;
   Take it to the Lord in prayer.
   Do thy friends despise, forsake thee?
   Take it to the Lord in prayer.
   In His arms He'll take and shield thee;
   Thou wilt find a solace there.

HAL·LEONARD
ACCORDION
PLAY·ALONG

The Accordion Play-Along series features custom accordion arrangements with CD tracks recorded by a live band (accordion, bass and drums). There are two audio tracks for each song – a full performance for listening, plus a separate backing track which lets you be the soloist! The CD is playable on any CD player, and is also enhanced so Mac and PC users can adjust the recording to any tempo without changing the pitch!

1. POLKA FAVORITES
arr. Gary Meisner

Beer Barrel Polka (Roll Out the Barrel) • Hoop-Dee-Doo • Hop-scotch Polka • Just Another Polka • Just Because • Pennsylvania Polka • Tic-Tock Polka • Too Fat Polka (She's Too Fat for Me).
00701705 Book/CD Pack.......................................$19.99

2. ALL-TIME HITS
arr. Gary Meisner

Edelweiss • Fly Me to the Moon (In Other Words) • I Left My Heart in San Francisco • It's a Small World • Moon River • More (Ti Guarderò Nel Cuore) • Poinciana (Song of the Tree) • When I'm Sixty-Four.
00701706 Book/CD Pack.......................................$19.99

3. CLASSIC SONGS
arr. Gary Meisner

Carnival of Venice • Ciribiribin • Come Back to Sorrento • Fascination (Valse Tzigane) • Funiculi, Funicula • I Love You Truly • In the Good Old Summertime • Melody of Love • Peg O' My Heart • When Irish Eyes Are Smiling.
00701707 Book/CD Pack.......................................$14.99

4. CHRISTMAS SONGS
arr. Gary Meisner

Frosty the Snow Man • Have Yourself a Merry Little Christmas • Here Comes Santa Claus (Right down Santa Claus Lane) • The Most Wonderful Time of the Year • Rudolph the Red-Nosed Reindeer • Santa Claus Is Comin' to Town • Silver Bells • Winter Wonderland.
00101770 Book/CD Pack.......................................$14.99

5. ITALIAN SONGS
arr. Gary Meisner

La Sorella • La Spagnola • Mattinata • 'O Sole Mio • Oh Marie • Santa Lucia • Tarantella • Vieni Sul Mar.
00101771 Book/CD Pack.......................................$14.99

Visit Hal Leonard online at **www.halleonard.com**

A COLLECTION OF ALL-TIME FAVORITES
FOR ACCORDION

ACCORDION FAVORITES
arr. Gary Meisner
16 all-time favorites, arranged for accordion, including: Can't Smile Without You • Could I Have This Dance • Endless Love • Memory • Sunrise, Sunset • I.O.U. • and more.
00359012..$12.99

ALL-TIME FAVORITES FOR ACCORDION
arr. Gary Meisner
20 must-know standards arranged for accordions. Includes: Ain't Misbehavin' • Autumn Leaves • Crazy • Hello, Dolly! • Hey, Good Lookin' • Moon River • Speak Softly, Love • Unchained Melody • The Way We Were • Zip-A-Dee-Doo-Dah • and more.
00311088..$12.99

THE BEATLES FOR ACCORDION
17 hits from the Lads from Liverpool have been arranged for accordion. Includes: All You Need Is Love • Eleanor Rigby • The Fool on the Hill • Here Comes the Sun • Hey Jude • In My Life • Let It Be • Ob-La-Di, Ob-La-Da • Penny Lane • When I'm Sixty-Four • Yesterday • and more.
00268724 ....$14.99

BROADWAY FAVORITES
arr. Ken Kotwitz
A collection of 17 wonderful show songs, including: Don't Cry for Me Argentina • Getting to Know You • If I Were a Rich Man • Oklahoma • People Will Say We're in Love • We Kiss in a Shadow.
00490157..$10.99

DISNEY SONGS FOR ACCORDION – 3RD EDITION
13 Disney favorites especially arranged for accordion, including: Be Our Guest • Beauty and the Beast • Can You Feel the Love Tonight • Chim Chim Cher-ee • It's a Small World • Let It Go • Under the Sea • A Whole New World • You'll Be in My Heart • Zip-A-Dee-Doo-Dah • and more!
00152508 ....$12.99

FIRST 50 SONGS YOU SHOULD PLAY ON THE ACCORDION
arr. Gary Meisner
If you're new to the accordion, you are probably eager to learn some songs. This book provides 50 simplified arrangements of must-know popular standards, folk songs and show tunes, including: All of Me • Beer Barrel Polka • Carnival of Venice • Edelweiss • Hava Nagila (Let's Be Happy) • Hernando's Hideaway • Jambalaya (On the Bayou) • Lady of Spain • Moon River • 'O Sole Mio • Sentimental Journey • Somewhere, My Love • That's Amore (That's Love) • Under Paris Skies • and more. Includes lyrics when applicable.
00250269 ....$16.99

FRENCH SONGS FOR ACCORDION
arr. Gary Meisner
A très magnifique collection of 17 French standards arranged for the accordion. Includes: Autumn Leaves • Beyond the Sea • C'est Magnifique • I Love Paris • La Marseillaise • Let It Be Me (Je T'appartiens) • Under Paris Skies • Watch What Happens • and more.
00311498..$10.99

HYMNS FOR ACCORDION
arr. Gary Meisner
24 treasured sacred favorites arranged for accordion, including: Amazing Grace • Beautiful Savior • Come, Thou Fount of Every Blessing • Crown Him with Many Crowns • Holy, Holy, Holy • It Is Well with My Soul • Just a Closer Walk with Thee • A Mighty Fortress Is Our God • Nearer, My God, to Thee • The Old Rugged Cross • Rock of Ages • What a Friend We Have in Jesus • and more.
00277160 ....$9.99

ITALIAN SONGS FOR ACCORDION
arr. Gary Meisner
17 favorite Italian standards arranged for accordion, including: Carnival of Venice • Ciribiribin • Come Back to Sorrento • Funiculi, Funicula • La donna è mobile • La Spagnola • 'O Sole Mio • Santa Lucia • Tarantella • and more.
00311089..$12.99

LATIN FAVORITES FOR ACCORDION
arr. Gary Meisner
20 Latin favorites, including: Bésame Mucho (Kiss Me Much) • The Girl from Ipanema • How Insensitive (Insensatez) • Perfidia • Spanish Eyes • So Nice (Summer Samba) • and more.
00310932..$14.99

THE FRANK MAROCCO ACCORDION SONGBOOK
This songbook includes arrangements and recordings of 15 standards and original songs from legendary jazz accordionist Frank Marocco, including: All the Things You Are • Autumn Leaves • Beyond the Sea • Moon River • Moonlight in Vermont • Stormy Weather (Keeps Rainin' All the Time) • and more!
00233441 Book/Online Audio..............$19.99

POP STANDARDS FOR ACCORDION
Arrangements of 20 Classic Songs
20 classic pop standards arranged for accordion are included in this collection: Annie's Song • Chances Are • For Once in My Life • Help Me Make It Through the Night • My Cherie Amour • Ramblin' Rose • (Sittin' On) The Dock of the Bay • That's Amore (That's Love) • Unchained Melody • and more.
00254822 ....$14.99

POLKA FAVORITES
arr. Kenny Kotwitz
An exciting new collection of 16 songs, including: Beer Barrel Polka • Liechtensteiner Polka • My Melody of Love • Paloma Blanca • Pennsylvania Polka • Too Fat Polka • and more.
00311573..$12.99

STAR WARS FOR ACCORDION
A dozen songs from the Star Wars franchise: The Imperial March (Darth Vader's Theme) • Luke and Leia • March of the Resistance • Princess Leia's Theme • Rey's Theme • Star Wars (Main Theme) • and more.
00157380 ....$14.99

TANGOS FOR ACCORDION
arr. Gary Meisner
Every accordionist needs to know some tangos! Here are 15 favorites: Amapola (Pretty Little Poppy) • Aquellos Ojos Verdes (Green Eyes) • Hernando's Hideaway • Jalousie (Jealousy) • Kiss of Fire • La Cumparsita (The Masked One) • Quizás, Quizás, Quizás (Perhaps, Perhaps, Perhaps) • The Rain in Spain • Tango of Roses • Whatever Lola Wants (Lola Gets) • and more!
00122252 ....$12.99

3-CHORD SONGS FOR ACCORDION
arr. Gary Meisner
Here are nearly 30 songs that are easy to play but still sound great! Includes: Amazing Grace • Can Can • Danny Boy • For He's a Jolly Good Fellow • He's Got the Whole World in His Hands • Just a Closer Walk with Thee • La Paloma Blanca (The White Dove) • My Country, 'Tis of Thee • Ode to Joy • Oh! Susanna • Yankee Doodle • The Yellow Rose of Texas • and more.
00312104 ....$12.99

LAWRENCE WELK'S POLKA FOLIO
More than 50 famous polkas, schottisches and waltzes arranged for piano and accordion, including: Blue Eyes • Budweiser Polka • Clarinet Polka • Cuckoo Polka • The Dove Polka • Draw One Polka • Gypsy Polka • Helena Polka • International Waltzes • Let's Have Another One • Schnitzelbank • Shuffle Schottische • Squeeze Box Polka • Waldteufel Waltzes • and more.
00123218..$14.99

HAL•LEONARD®
Visit Hal Leonard Online at
www.halleonard.com

Learn to Play Today
with folk music instruction from Hal Leonard

Hal Leonard Bagpipe Method

The Hal Leonard Bagpipe Method is designed for anyone just learning to play the Great Highland bagpipes. This comprehensive and easy-to-use beginner's guide serves as an introduction to the bagpipe chanter. It includes access to online video lessons with demonstrations of all the examples in the book! Lessons include: the practice chanter, the Great Highland Bagpipe scale, bagpipe notation, proper technique, grace-noting, embellishments, playing and practice tips, traditional tunes, buying a bagpipe, and much more!
00102521 Book/Online Video $16.99

Hal Leonard Banjo Method – Second Edition

Authored by Mac Robertson, Robbie Clement & Will Schmid. This innovative method teaches 5-string, bluegrass style. The method consists of two instruction books and two cross-referenced supplement books that offer the beginner a carefully-paced and interest-keeping approach to the bluegrass style.
00699500 Book 1 Only..........................$9.99
00695101 Book 1 with Online Audio..............$17.99
00699502 Book 2 Only..........................$9.99
00696056 Book 2 with Online Audio..............$17.99

Hal Leonard Brazilian Guitar Method

by Carlos Arana

This book uses popular Brazilian songs to teach you the basics of the Brazilian guitar style and technique. Learn to play in the styles of Joao Gilberto, Luiz Bonfá, Baden Powell, Dino Sete Cordas, Joao Basco, and many others! Includes 33 demonstration tracks.
00697415 Book/Online Audio $17.99

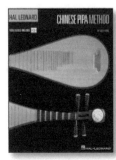

Hal Leonard Chinese Pipa Method

by Gao Hong

This easy-to-use book serves as an introduction to the Chinese pipa and its techniques. Lessons include: tuning • Western & Chinese notation basics • left and right hand techniques • positions • tremolo • bending • vibrato and overtones • classical pipa repertoire • popular Chinese folk tunes • and more!
00121398 Book/Online Video $19.99

Hal Leonard Dulcimer Method – Second Edition

by Neal Hellman

A beginning method for the Appalachian dulcimer with a unique new approach to solo melody and chord playing. Includes tuning, modes and many beautiful folk songs all demonstrated on the audio accompaniment. Music and tablature.
00699289 Book.................$12.99
00697230 Book/Online Audio..........................$19.99

Hal Leonard Flamenco Guitar Method

by Hugh Burns

Traditional Spanish flamenco song forms and classical pieces are used to teach you the basics of the style and technique in this book. Lessons cover: strumming, picking and percussive techniques • arpeggios • improvisation • fingernail tips • capos • and much more. Includes flamenco history and a glossary.
00697363 Book/Online Audio $17.99

Hal Leonard Irish Bouzouki Method

by Roger Landes

This comprehensive method focuses on teaching the basics of the instrument as well as accompaniment techniques for a variety of Irish song forms. It covers: playing position • tuning • picking & strumming patterns • learning the fretboard • accompaniment styles • double jigs, slip jigs & reels • drones • counterpoint • arpeggios • playing with a capo • traditional Irish songs • and more.
00696348 Book/Online Audio $12.99

Hal Leonard Mandolin Method – Second Edition

Noted mandolinist and teacher Rich Del Grosso has authored this excellent mandolin method that features great playable tunes in several styles (bluegrass, country, folk, blues) in standard music notation and tablature. The audio features play-along duets.
00699296 Book.................$10.99
00695102 Book/Online Audio..........................$16.99

Hal Leonard Oud Method

by John Bilezikjian

This book teaches the fundamentals of standard Western music notation in the context of oud playing. It also covers: types of ouds, tuning the oud, playing position, how to string the oud, scales, chords, arpeggios, tremolo technique, studies and exercises, songs and rhythms from Armenia and the Middle East, and 25 audio tracks for demonstration and play along.
00695836 Book/Online Audio $14.99

Hal Leonard Sitar Method

by Josh Feinberg

This beginner's guide serves as an introduction to sitar and its technique, as well as the practice, theory, and history of raga music. Lessons include: tuning • postures • right- and left-hand technique • Indian notation • raga forms; melodic patterns • bending strings • hammer-ons, pull-offs, and slides • changing strings • and more!
00696613 Book/Online Audio $16.99
00198245 Book/Online Media $19.99

Hal Leonard Ukulele Method

by Lil' Rev

This comprehensive and easy-to-use beginner's guide by acclaimed performer and uke master Lil' Rev includes many fun songs of different styles to learn and play. Includes: types of ukuleles, tuning, music reading, melody playing, chords, strumming, scales, tremolo, music notation and tablature, a variety of music styles, ukulele history and much more.
00695847 Book 1 Only.......................$8.99
00695832 Book 1 with Online Audio..............$12.99
00695948 Book 2 Only.......................$7.99
00695949 Book 2 with Online Audio..............$11.99

HAL•LEONARD®

Visit Hal Leonard Online at
www.halleonard.com

Prices and availability subject to change without notice.

0522
003